BEING FAITHFUL
to Your
FUTURE
SPOUSE

Faithfulness Begins *Before* You Meet

TOM HOUCK

WINTERS
PUBLISHING

www.winterspublishing.com
812-663-4948

Being Faithful to Your Future Spouse: Faithfulness Begins Before You Meet

© 2012 Tom Houck

Published by:
Winters Publishing
P.O. Box 501
Greensburg, IN 47240
812-663-4948
www.winterspublishing.com

Cover design by Kelly Lynn Sexton

ISBN 10: 1-883651-55-7
ISBN 13: 978-1-883651-55-8

Library of Congress Control Number: 2012948260

Printed in the United States of America

ACKNOWLEDGMENTS

I would like to thank first and foremost my Lord and Savior Jesus Christ who mercifully rescued me from the world's destructive system of relating to the opposite gender. Next, I extend my most sincere gratitude to my wonderful wife, Lisa, who spent countless hours over the years helping me in so many ways. She was always there to encourage me through my writing endeavors and was a tremendous support by her like-minded beliefs. We are co-laborers together in this ministry.

I must thank the people who helped organize and develop my thoughts into written material. I would like to thank Barbara Winslow Robidoux who helped me immensely with her editing skills. Also, I must thank the many people who fed me valuable input after reading the many versions of this book along the way. Thanks to Harold Mally and his entire family whose input and support have been so valuable to me in developing this book. A special thanks to Pastor Eric Burd who also took the time to read my manuscript and provide valuable input.

TABLE OF CONTENTS

FOREWORD

As a singles pastor of fourteen years, I spent a lot of time immersed in the world of single adults. When I first began pastoring I was newly married, so what it was like to be single was fresh in my mind. I understood the process God had brought me through when He transformed my life from worldly singleness to godly singleness. It didn't take me long to see that what I would be spending most of my time doing as pastor would be helping the single adults to deal with their unwanted baggage of the past and misconceptions about singleness. I was convinced this would be my lifelong calling and never imagined ministering to any other group of people.

The first time I was asked to reach outside of the single adult arena was to speak to a group of high school students at a local Christian school. I felt as though I was in familiar territory as the message remained the same. I didn't see much of a difference between speaking to the teens or speaking to single adults. But then I was asked to share my message with elementary school children. As I prepared for this meeting I was forced to think of romantic relationships from a child's perspective, not my familiar, single adult's view. The major difference I noticed was there was no need to address how to deal with past baggage in this group. My realization was, "If children were taught this message early, they wouldn't have to have their minds renewed later in life."

The concept was good, but after a couple of meetings with this age group I discovered that it would be less fruitful to share this information with children if their parents were not on the same page. This insight inspired me to reach out to parents in order to teach children God's plan for singleness. My first book *Parenting for Purity* was then published to meet that need.

It has been six years since *Parenting for Purity* was published.

Since then I have learned a lot. I have paid attention to how people have received the information in that book. It has been overwhelmingly positive, yet I have seen where people have misinterpreted what I was saying. I have made changes and clarifications in this book to make the communication of my faith effectual.

This book is not meant to be an exhaustive study on this subject, but rather an overview to entice its readers to study further.

PART I

ISSUES OF THE HEART

CHAPTER 1

PREPARE TO BE A BLESSING

Predictable

Many years ago I ran my first twenty-six mile marathon. A lot of training and preparation was needed to properly prepare to run that distance. Part of that preparation was to think ahead to what obstacles I would be facing during the race. One of the obstacles I knew I would face was the temptation to quit and not finish the race. Therefore, when I was practicing, I not only had to get in shape physically, I also had to train in a certain way to develop a "no quit" attitude when I ran.

One of the decisions I made was to complete whatever goal I set for myself prior to beginning each training run. If I was planning to run six, eight, or even twelve miles that day, I didn't allow myself the luxury of lessening the distance while I was running. I knew if I did, I would be practicing quitting and I never wanted to do that. I'm pleased to be able to say that the training worked. In fact, after completing my very first marathon, I went home, took a nap, got up, and ran six more miles. The accomplishments of that day were the direct results of the preparation for it. Practicing not quitting had really made a difference. The lesson learned here is, whatever a person practices usually indicates what their future behavior will be.

In the Parable of the Talents, Jesus explained the blessing of being faithful over what we already have been given. *"His master said to him, 'Well done, good and faithful servant; you have been **faithful** over a **little**, I will set you over **much**; enter into the joy of your master"* (Matthew 25:21 RSV, emphasis added). Never should anyone fool themselves, or be fooled by others, to believe that their thoughts and behaviors of today will not have an effect on their tomorrows. That is why I must discuss with you what a person should do prior to marriage. The biblical truth is that what a person does *prior* to marriage really makes a *difference* in what they do *after* they are married. This principle is best described in Galatians 6:7 (NKJV) *"Do not be deceived, God is not mocked; for whatever a man sows, that he will also reap."*

If you want to find out where a train is going, all you have to do is look further down the tracks to determine where that train will take you. Sometimes we ignore a comparatively lesser degree of a certain sin, believing that will not harm us. But, those are the sins that at the beginning of the train's departure do not seem so bad. Then, as the train continues toward its final destination, those sins become progressively worse. So what can we do to not end up committing sins that we are absolutely against? We need to make the connection between those smaller sins that lead us to the greater ones. It's all about prevention! We must not allow the lesser degree of that sin that leads to the major ones.

We must deal with all of our sins at their root and understand this is a heart issue. *"But among you there must not be even a **hint** of sexual immorality, or of any kind of impurity, or of greed, because these are improper for God's holy people"* (Ephesians 5:3, emphasis added). Not even a hint means we should stay away from the train station that has the train that we shouldn't be on! Some people deceive themselves by thinking that, rather than staying off that train, they can learn how to be an expert in jumping off a moving train instead. This is a bad and painful strategy. If our heart is right, then we would not want anything to do with even those "lesser" sins. After all, sin is sin.

Relationships Prior to Marriage

Most of the boyfriend/girlfriend relationships we see today do not match the type of relationship needed to translate into a successful marriage. Those relationships are usually not created for the right purpose, nor do they contain the right kind of preparation or practice. Going from these types of relationships into a marriage relationship is extremely difficult. As a result of this inconsistency, there ends up being a lot of repair work that needs to be done after the marriage ceremony. If a person really loves his/her future spouse, then certainly that person would not want to conduct any relationships prior to marriage in a way that would cause them problems after their wedding.

Dating, the way it usually takes place today, is nothing more than divorce practice. Often, people create temporary dating relationships to interview candidates to see which one will qualify for a permanent relationship. They *test* people out to see if he or she will meet their expectations. If an individual doesn't, they cast them aside, and then it's on to the next candidate. This concept, often repeated several times, makes a person an expert at temporary commitments. Then, after getting married, he/she is likely to also treat that relationship as temporary, with its continuation based on whether their mate is currently meeting expectations or not. If their spouse slips-up, even one time, then it's easy to fall back on their old habit of temporary trial relationships by moving on to the next one. This type of relationship is unstable and unhealthy because it lacks real commitment. Since God intends marriage to be a permanent commitment, a person cannot prepare for that by practicing with a bunch of temporary relationships.

It is an illogical concept to believe that a person can form a temporary relationship to try another person out for a marriage relationship, when marriage requires a permanent commitment to be experienced correctly. A person cannot "try out" marriage, in the same way they cannot try out a relationship with Jesus. Both require a wholehearted commitment **first**, before that relationship can even begin. That's why it is no surprise to see that the statistics show that those who attempt to try out marriage without the permanent marriage commitment end up having a higher rate of divorce!

Faithfulness to a Future Spouse

A major contradiction found in those relationships that do not match what is required in marriage is faithfulness. Faithfulness is the lifetime commitment to remain *emotionally* and *physically* devoted to only one person, and is one of the requirements of marriage that should be practiced prior to entering it. However, due to the double standard created by our society, it has become acceptable to believe that following that type of commitment to one person throughout one's single years doesn't matter, and it is not something to be concerned with.

Under that worldly standard, it really doesn't matter how many boyfriends/girlfriends a person has before he/she gets married. But the truth is, having a boyfriend/girlfriend relationship with someone you will never marry is contrary to being faithful to the one you will eventually marry. Why? Because you are giving away pieces of your heart by creating memories of emotional and physical attachments. Unfortunately, the memories from those attachments, if not repented of, can afterward be brought into a future marriage as harmful baggage. It is easier to never create those memories in the first place, than it is to forget them. For this reason a boyfriend/girlfriend relationship should be reserved only for a person's future spouse. When I say boyfriend/girlfriend relationship, I mean a relationship with romantic interests. It is much different than having a boy or girl who is your friend.

What if? ....

For anyone who has **already** been involved in a relationship not ordained by God, His best for them is to acknowledge that relationship as being harmful to a future marriage, even if they didn't know at the time it was wrong. Then commit from now on to have only one romantic relationship. Don't add to that mistake by condemning yourself. That won't help! Not only is it impossible to change the past, it's foolish to try. You are, however, responsible for your future. *Never* should anyone think, "I have already blown it, so what does it really matter if I do the wrong thing again?" Keep in mind that with each mistake we make there is more damage done. Always limit your mistakes and make the best of whatever situation you find yourself in. *"But God, who is rich in mercy, because of His great love with which He loved us, even when we were dead in trespasses, made us alive together with Christ (by grace you have been saved)"* (Ephesians 2:4-5 NKJV). It's never too late to commit to be faithful from now on!

When to be Faithful

Currently, many people have a detrimental belief concerning **when** a person should begin to be faithful to their future spouse. There is always a period of time prior to marriage when a person has no idea who their mate is going to be. Many people use this fact of not knowing who that particular person will be as a seemingly legitimate reason to lessen their commitment to them. Those who think this way do not believe it is necessary to have the same level of commitment to be faithful to their future spouse, whom they haven't met up to this point, as they would have if they already knew them. But the truth is, the level of commitment both before and after meeting a future spouse should be identical. Not knowing who their future spouse is going to be does not give anyone the freedom to not save all of their romantic emotions and affections for that future spouse. *To be **faithful** to their spouse, a person should be faithful both before and after they meet them.* Proverbs 31:12 gives us an encouragement to live this way, *"She brings him good, not harm, all the days of her life."* It says **all** the days of her life, not just the days after she meets him.

Looking at this from a natural perspective we can see that, depending on someone's age, their future spouse already exists. There is a person to be faithful to right now! For example, if a child is four years old and his/her future spouse is the same age or four years younger, that spouse has already been born. Just because they don't know who that person is doesn't mean he or she doesn't exist.

Contributing to a Divorce Epidemic

This trend of having boyfriend/girlfriend relationships that are inconsistent with the marriage relationship has caused many marriages to fail and has put our country in the midst of a divorce epidemic. I say *epidemic*, because we have had a fifty-percent divorce rate for more than thirty years. Since 1974, there have been over one million divorces each and every year. According to Barna's Research, out of the fifty-percent of marriages that do end in divorce, Christians are involved in slightly over half of them. There is obviously something wrong that needs to be corrected! Unless Christians change from imitating the world's way of conducting their relationships, continuing to neglect what is necessary for a successful marriage, we can expect to see the epidemic continue. In order to see the epidemic end, we must see a significant increase in the number of boyfriend/girlfriend relationships that **match** what is required to have a successful marriage.

Unfortunately, many have misdiagnosed this divorce epidemic, and have declared that the reason for this is that the institution of marriage itself doesn't always work. But, the truth is that marriage, the way God designed it, always works. It's only when we modify or ignore His design that marriage is weakened. So, when considering the drastic failure rate, our conclusion must be that many people are not following God's original plan for marriage. **Therefore, the only true solution to this crisis is following that plan**.

Please believe that I am not here to condemn anyone who has already been divorced. Let's not concern ourselves for the moment with what has happened in the past. Again, not only is it impossible to change the past, it's foolish to try. This is a from-now-on-message. My desire is to see divorce **prevented** in the lives of those of you who will one day be married.

Teaching prevention requires that I share this from a perfect world perspective. This is how a parent would teach a child who has no history of unbiblical relationships. However, I cannot discuss how to prevent divorce without first talking about what caused the epidemic we now face. I do this with full understanding that, while

I am pointing out how to make corrections to the path our society has taken, I will more than likely bring up what may have caused the problem for those who have already been divorced, possibly causing them shame or hurt. Discussing mistakes that people have already made is an unavoidable necessity if we want to prevent those same mistakes from being made in the lives of others. However, I will not neglect those who have made mistakes in the past. The next chapter will be dedicated to those who suffer pain or embarrassment caused by those mistakes.

CHAPTER 2

HELP! I AM NOT PERFECT

I realize that in today's world many of us have violated biblical principles concerning male/female relationships in our past. That does not mean that anyone who has made mistakes in this area is now permanently disqualified from participating in God's wonderful plan of male and female relationships that lead to marriage. The good news is that everything the Bible has to say about relationships is not limited only to those who have already done well in this area; it **is also for those of us who have not**. Actually, we who have already made mistakes should be more desperate to follow God's plan. Because, by committing those errors, we have chosen a more difficult path for ourselves by not following God in the first place. While not impossible to make corrections in this area, it will just be difficult and will require us to fight even more battles. However, keep in mind that the alternative to not making these corrections is much worse! Therefore, the battles will be well worth it.

This book is not only a lesson on how not to make mistakes, but also a story of God's grace being able to redeem those of us who have already committed those sins. The Gospel story describes God's desire and ability to save even those who are extremely and utterly lost. There isn't any person who is beyond redemption and restoration, so no one has to be left out. But, if we truly want to be dependent upon God's grace, we must learn how He wants us to manage our past and how to view others who also have missed the mark. We must not allow ourselves to fall into the trap of using condemnation or being judgmental.

Philippians 3:13-14 (RSV) puts it this way, *"Brethren, I do not consider that I have made it my own; but one thing I do, **forgetting** what **lies behind** and straining **forward** to what **lies ahead**, I press on toward the goal for the prize of the **upward** call of God in Christ Jesus"* (emphasis added). This is not offered as an excuse to ignore dealing with our failures. On the contrary, we must deal with them. To be truly set free from our mistakes, we must admit and take responsibility for those sins and then receive God's forgiveness. After admitting what we have done is wrong, and repenting from that, we must then not define ourselves by that wrongdoing. We must not let our past failures keep us from becoming the person God has called us to be.

Condemnation Has No Value

Even though God is unwilling to give up on imperfect people, there are many who do not share His compassion. They prefer to treat others with judgment and condemnation. In fact, many intentionally use condemnation in an attempt to manipulate others into doing what is right. Sadly, this concept is a highly ineffective means of motivating people toward repentance. Instead, we are told in Romans 2:4 that, *"it is His kindness that leads us toward repentance."* Always keep in mind that God's grace is the best motivator. *"For the grace of God that brings salvation has appeared to all men. It **teaches us to say "No"** to ungodliness and worldly passions, and to live self-controlled, upright and godly lives in this present age"* (Titus 2:11, emphasis added).

There are always those who prefer to stand by looking for ways to find fault in others, in order to condemn them in a futile attempt to build their own self-esteem by making themselves feel superior. Those who think this way incorrectly view life as a contest to see who is a "better" Christian. Unfortunately, some who still struggle with guilt over past sins become inappropriately intimidated by judgmental Christians. They fall victim to this arrogant plot and easily accept condemnation from those so-called "better" Christians. The truth is that Christianity is not a contest that can be won individually by competing against one another—true victory can only come by winning collectively, together as a whole, along with others. We excel by living in a way that will benefit others by building them up, not tearing them down. A self-centered Christianity is not Christianity at all.

While it is never my intention to purposely condemn other people for their past sins, I do, however, believe it is impossible to teach biblical truth to a multitude of people and not have someone feel condemned or judged because of guilt over a previously committed sin. This is why I need to address this issue in the likely event that someone would feel condemned or judged over something I might say. My desire for them is to be aware of how he/she can escape such condemnation and receive the blessings of God's truth.

Some, in a failed attempt to solve this dilemma of unintended condemnation, have resorted to creating a theology that bypasses any biblical message that might cause a person to feel condemned or judged. Even though there probably will be some who will feel condemned, it would be wrong to shy away from declaring God's standard. Now it would be great if that never happened, but concern for people's feelings can't become a higher priority than sharing the truth found in God's Word.

Reasons Condemnation Comes

When a person does something wrong, that is one mistake. When they do something wrong and condemn themselves over it, that is two mistakes. Therefore, self-condemnation becomes a stumbling block that must be removed. If we understand that there is a **difference** between conviction and self-condemnation, we will be better equipped to handle our mistakes and not make them worse.

When a person with a healthy conscience commits a sin, conviction comes immediately as a result of that sin to alert us to a wrong we have done. We feel guilty. The proper response to that conviction should be repentance and asking forgiveness from God as soon as the conviction comes.

Self-condemnation, on the other hand, occurs when a person **does not** respond immediately or completely to that conviction with repentance or accepting forgiveness from God. They either know they should repent but choose not to, or they **refuse** to be unconditionally forgiven. As a result, self-condemnation comes from lingering in conviction without the proper or complete actions being taken. *Condemnation is living in a state of perpetual conviction and is an unbiblical response to sin that only compounds the problem.*

In light of God's costly provision of Christ's shed blood for the forgiveness of sins, we must be compelled to receive that forgiveness—we should never give ourselves any other option. Unfortunately, there are many Christians who try to earn forgiveness by punishing themselves for their sins, rather than relying on the fact that Jesus has already taken the punishment for us. However, it is impossible to **earn** forgiveness from God. Being forgiven by God is a miracle that can only happen because of what Jesus has done at the cross. Therefore, our dependency should always be on Him. We should always be on guard of developing a "Never mind, God, I will do it myself" attitude.

Some incorrectly treat condemnation as though it is a dear friend. They falsely believe they are being virtuous by supposedly humbling themselves with self-abasement. They reject God's plan on the basis that they are not worthy of Christ's amazing grace. While that is true, it is prideful to think that anyone's sacrifice could be a substitute for our Lord's, or that it could even come close to accomplishing what was done at the cross. We must be able to admit that it is impossible to free ourselves from the snare of sin. Either Christ's sacrifice for the forgiveness of sins was enough or it wasn't. I believe it was more than enough for even the worst of sins.

In 1 John 1:9 we read there is nothing unjust about God forgiving our sins. *"If we confess our sins, He is **faithful** and **just** to forgive us our sins and to **cleanse** us from all unrighteousness"* (NKJV, emphasis added). We are not asking God to do anything additional for us, it has already been done, the price has *already* been paid at the cross. Without Christ's shed blood on the cross it would not be just for God to forgive us only because we repented. A price had to be paid for our sins. Romans 6:23 tells us, *"For the wages of sin is death, but the gift of God is eternal life in Christ Jesus our Lord."* Once that price was paid, our being forgiven does not inconvenience God in any way! He desires for us to receive His forgiveness because of its benefits. 1 John 1:9 points out one of the benefits of forgiveness—the cleansing of all unrighteousness. The purpose of that forgiveness is not to help us get away with something wrong; it is to cleanse us so that we don't have to repeat that particular sin. Forgiveness from God allows a person to go and sin no more. (See John 8:1-11).

Check the Source

Sometimes people dismiss any responsibility of feeling condemnation by blaming others for their guilt when, in reality, other people have only inadvertently reminded them of guilt that has previously existed. The reason they do this is so they do not have to deal with their own guilt by assigning the blame to others. It is important to realize that being judged or receiving condemnation can come from one of two places—either from others, or from within. Both are very real! The most responsible thing to do if you ever feel condemned over something is to first raise a red flag, and then honestly seek the source of that condemnation. Never automatically assign blame to someone else. Admit that it is possible that you may be bringing that condemnation upon yourself.

Being judged or condemned does not always come from other people, such as a teaching a person has heard or from a conversation with someone. Even though it may truly feel like you are being judged or condemned at the time, it is often based on how the hearer has applied what is being said to his/her own life, so they become offended. It is often the way a person perceives how others view them; they feel as though others condemn them. While this is sometimes true, it is not always the case. Jesus instructs us in Luke 8:18 on the importance of hearing correctly: *"Therefore take heed __how you hear__"* (NKJV, emphasis added). Everyone needs to take responsibility for *how* they apply what they hear so they don't miss the intention of what is actually being said.

Another way condemnation can come from within is experienced by those who are convinced that the life he/she is currently living is the standard that all should live by. So when they encounter someone who is living or teaching a higher standard than the one he/she is living, they feel as though they are being judged, condemned, or seen as inferior by others. Such people have become so self-aware that they think someone else is judging them, even when they are not being judged. Either through pride, or unwillingness to change, they have convinced themselves to reject any standard other than the one they are currently living under. They use that feeling of judgment or condemnation as justification for their rejection of that higher standard. This serves as a means of deflecting their attention away from their own guilt by placing attention onto someone else.

It is God's intent that we should encourage one another with our lifestyle. When we see someone else living in closer fellowship with God, we should be convicted by that and desire to live that way ourselves. If we do not respond to that conviction, then that unacted upon conviction turns into condemnation, as I stated earlier. We are warned in Hebrews 3:7-8, 15, and 4:7, that when we hear the Holy Spirit speaking to us we should do as He says right away. *"Today, when you hear his voice, do not harden your hearts."* It is to our detriment to not respond immediately to the conviction of sin. If we respond immediately and completely, it will keep us from self-condemnation.

As Christians we must be ready and able to receive God's truth, regardless of it being contrary to our past. We must be able to apply it correctly and accept the responsibility of admitting when we have done something wrong, without using our sin as a weapon of condemnation against ourselves. We must not let our past paralyze us to the point that we cannot move forward. We must realize that our past is over and we cannot change it. We must, however, receive forgiveness and change whatever belief originally caused the problem in the first place. We must see it as a second chance that sets us free to not repeat that mistake; and to make that change in our beliefs so as to not pass our sin to others, but instead we must be able to bless them with God's unalterable truth.

CHAPTER 3

FOLLOWING INSTRUCTIONS

Worldly Christian Relationships

W hy do Christians have the same divorce rate as non-believers? For the most part, it's because the beliefs and behaviors found in "Christian dating" today are often not much different than secular dating. Those similarities exist because, too often, Christians copy the world's system and then try to "Christianize" it. What I mean by "Christianize" is to remove some of what is sinful and then call the entire practice good. What they don't seem to understand is that even though they take a worldly standard and *attempt* to clean it up, it still ends up being a worldly standard.

The idea that Christian and secular relationships can be conducted the same way is definitely not a biblical concept. First Thessalonians 4:4-5 (RSV) tells us there is a major difference between the two when it says, "*that each one of you know how to take a wife* [literally meaning to acquire a wife] *for himself in **holiness and honor**, not in the **passion of lust** like heathen who do not know God;*" (emphasis added). The two approaches that are mentioned here are totally opposite and therefore vastly different ways of conducting a relationship. God's way is with holiness and honor, and the godless' way is done in lust.

Unfortunately, Christians often create boyfriend/girlfriend relationships independent from God's input. They create those relationships when they want to, the way they want to, and with the person they want to; then, only *later,* do they ask God to bless that relationship. The problem with this scenario is that they did not seek God's involvement in important decisions that needed to be made prior to the start of that relationship. Then, after making those decisions without God's input, they are basically asking Him to please make the results of their previous decisions succeed, despite the fact they didn't believe His opinion was valuable enough to seek from the very beginning. Decisions have consequences! If a person wants good consequences, then he/she must make the right choices. If that person would have sought and followed God's guidance from the very beginning, the relationship would already be blessed.

God's influence should be included in every decision, in every step of the process, and most importantly, in the beginning stages. *"Unless the LORD builds the house, its builders labor in vain"* (Psalm 127:1). A commonly understood truth that every respectable home builder knows is that the beginning stage of the construction process is extremely critical. If the foundation is inaccurately laid, then problems will arise throughout the entire building process. The same holds true when one is building a relationship with another person.

Marriage is a relationship that God takes very seriously. I can say that because it is the **only** relationship between two human beings that He compares to the relationship between Christ and the Church (See Ephesians 5:22-33). Unfortunately, people have trivialized marriage to the point that it has lost its true meaning. It has lost its significance because of a shifting of priorities. There is a greater tendency to see couples trying to add God to their relationship, rather than Him being the reason for it. Whether they realize it, or are willing to admit it, life is all about God. All marriage related problems can be traced back to ignoring this one issue.

Instructions Are Needed

Parents today must deliberately parent their children in the area of male/female relationships rather than parenting by default; in other words whatever happens, happens. Many Christian parents falsely believe that by discipling their children in other areas of conduct they have covered male/female relationships. That's like teaching English and geography while believing that a person will also learn math in the process; each is a uniquely different subject.

We learn in 1 Thessalonians 4:3-6 that we need instructions for dealing with male/female relationships and are given some reasons why we do. No one should ever think or pretend to be above needing those instructions. It is necessary to learn them, because this type of information never comes as the result of our natural human instinct. Because it doesn't come naturally, we must look to God for divine help. We must, therefore, purposely have our minds renewed by the truth on this topic found in God's Word.

We can begin reading about this concept in verse three, *"It is God's will that you should be sanctified: that you should avoid sexual immorality."* We could stop the discussion right there if it were true that we could just tell someone not to be immoral before marriage. If that admonishment were sufficient, there would be no reason for further information. But it obviously isn't, because it goes on to say in verses four through six, *"that each one of you know how* [or learn] *to take a wife* [literally meaning to acquire a wife] *for himself in holiness and honor, not in the passion of lust like heathen who do not know God;"* (RSV) *"That no man go beyond and defraud his brother in any matter:"* (KJV). Verse four implies that we don't *already* know how to acquire a wife, but that the knowledge has to be learned. If it is not learned, then the consequences of verses five and six—relationships that resemble those who don't know God, and the defrauding of our brothers and sisters—should be expected.

You probably have noticed that I used three different translations to quote 1 Thessalonians 4:3-6—NIV for verse three, RSV for verses four and five, and KJV for verse six. I carefully chose the version that would most accurately represent the original text and is the most easily understood for each of those verses. Every translation has its pluses along with its minuses, and I have no problem using a translation that is not perfect. Please remember that when I use a verse from a certain translation it is not an endorsement of that entire translation, only that particular verse.

One of the keys to understanding how all of these verses in 1 Thessalonians 4:3-6 fit together is found in verse four, but it can literally get lost in the translation. All of the different translations of these verses contain an element of truth to them; I am not saying that any one of them is totally wrong, the problem is not every one of them bring out the truth in its entirety.

In 1 Thessalonians 4:4 there are three Greek words used in the original text—*ktaomai, heautou,* and *skeuos*. Here is that verse in the KJV showing the Greek words, shown in superscript, that were used to translate this verse. The translated phrase comes first, followed by the Greek word that it was translated from. That every one *hekastos* of you *hymōn* should know *eidō* how to possess *ktaomai* his *heautou* vessel *skeuos* in *en* sanctification *hagiasmos* and *kai* honour *timē*.

Ktaomai and *skeuos* are the significant words we need to understand to give us the proper meaning of this verse. *Heautou* is a reflexive pronoun of the third person, typically translated as *himself, themselves, yourselves,* or *ourselves*. The NKJV, NASB, and NAU all translate those three words into the phrase, "possess his own vessel." The KJV says, "possess his vessel," and the RSV translates it, "to take a wife." The NIV translated it, "his own body" which has a completely different meaning than the other versions. However, there is a footnote given in the NIV that says, "Or learn how to live with his own wife, or learn to acquire a wife." One of the common threads between all of these translations is the word vessel, although it is only used in the footnote in the NIV.

The word that is most often translated as vessel is the Greek word *skeuos* (skyoo'-os) which means of uncertain affinity; a vessel, implement, equipment or apparatus (literally or figuratively [specifically, a wife as contributing to the usefulness of the husband]. The Greek word *skeuos* is also found in 1 Peter 3:7 where it is used to refer to wives as vessels. Therefore, all indications point to wife as being the proper translation of that word.

Further evidence of translating *skeuos* into the word wife is found in the context in which the word is used. The Greek word *ktaomai* (ktah'-om-ahee) which means: to get, i.e. acquire (by any means; own) is used before the word *skeuos*. When those two words are used in combination it would not make any sense to translate the word *skeuos* as your own body, since a person cannot acquire themselves. You can, however, acquire a wife. My conclusion is verse four is referring to a wife, not to us as individuals, as it does in the NIV. Therefore, I believe that the RSV is the most reflective of the original translation, because it translates it, "to take a wife."

Let's return to the beginning of 1 Thessalonians 4:3-6 in our study of everyone's need to learn how to acquire a wife. Here we are given an admonition of God's insistence upon us to do four specific things. Verse three begins with, "*It is God's will*"; in other words, this is what God wants. Then in verses three through six He tells us what it is that He requires, each item beginning with the word *that*. God wants **that** we should be sanctified, **that** we should avoid sexual immorality, **that** each of us should know how to take a wife [or acquire a wife], **that** no man cross the boundary that keeps us from defrauding our brother in any matter.

Here is the list of what God wants:

1. **That** we should be sanctified.

2. **That** we should avoid sexual immorality.

3. **That** each of us should know how to take a wife [or acquire a wife].

4. **That** no man cross the boundary that keeps us from defrauding our brother in any matter.

It is crucial that we understand how these four parts are linked together. Notice that each of the first three items rely upon the fulfillment of the following item. What God wants is for us to first be sanctified. Sanctification is the setting apart of one's self to be used by God (See 2 Timothy 2:20-21). But, if we want to be sanctified, then we must secondly avoid immorality. If we want to avoid immorality, then we must thirdly learn and follow God's plan for taking a wife. If we want to follow God's plan for taking a wife, then fourthly, we can't go beyond the boundary God has placed between the brother/sister relationships and a marriage relationship, thereby defrauding our brother/sister.

This becomes increasingly vital as society has continued to go further and further down the path of family destruction. It is not like it was when those of us who are older grew up. It is much worse. Children today must be thoroughly equipped for the onslaught of immoral anti-family values. They must be discipled by their parents on how to be faithful to their future spouse.

Obstacles to Receiving Biblical Truth

For some parents, what I have to say may not be how your marriage began. That does not mean you're a bad person, or that you're married to the wrong person. I am not intending to judge or condemn parents for something in their past they can no longer change. I am, however, asking that you examine your beliefs, not for the purpose of condemning yourself, but for the purpose of improving your beliefs so you will be able to instruct your children and lead them into the best possible biblical direction.

Sadly, one of the greatest obstacles to promoting biblical relationships comes from parents who are unwilling to receive biblical instructions about boyfriend/girlfriend relationships for their child. Rather than accepting biblical truth, they rely on their own life as the **ultimate standard**. Upon hearing God's truth about relationships, they immediately begin to compare it to their own experience and, if it doesn't match, they incorrectly reject God's truth, and due to pride, elevate their own experience above that truth. As a result, parents often excuse a child's wrongdoing by rationalizing it with an "I did that, and I'm okay" attitude. (This seems to be more of a problem with those who have incorrectly believed that by following *some* of God's ways, they falsely believe they have followed *all* of His ways perfectly. They don't seem to understand that partial obedience doesn't justify any part of their unbiblical behavior.) It is a parent's responsibility to judge any standard by what is written in the Bible and not become so partial to personal experience that he/she is unwilling to accept the truth the Bible presents.

Proverbs 10:17 puts it this way, *"He who heeds **discipline** shows the way to **life**, but whoever ignores correction leads others **astray"*** (emphasis added). Discipline doesn't always mean punishment. Jesus' twelve disciples were not the twelve punished people. Discipline is putting into practice what the Bible has instructed and corrected us on. As parents, if we don't follow God's Word, we will ultimately lead our children astray, and we never want to do that.

Unfortunately, parents who are unwilling to admit past mistakes will ultimately consider what is wrong to be right. This is how sin gets passed down from generation to generation and ends up being repeated. Think of it this way: Pride is the glue that sin sticks to. If there have been mistakes that you have made in your past, it is beneficial to humbly admit those sins were wrong, repent from them, ask God's forgiveness, and do not linger in self-condemnation after that. (See chapter two for complete details.) Ultimately, as parents, we want our children to learn from our mistakes and not repeat them, and for them to experience God's best in all areas.

Parents must become major contributors in discipling their children in godly relationships. This is the best way to create a drastic increase in the number of people conducting their relationships prior to marriage in a way that is consistent with the marriage relationship. Parents who raise their children with these biblical values will prevent future problems, rather than having to face the more difficult process of replacing any previously learned unbiblical values with biblical ones later in their child's life.

PART II

SEVEN BELIEFS NEEDED TO BE FAITHFUL TO YOUR FUTURE SPOUSE

CHAPTER 4

GOD'S SPECIFIC PERSON FOR YOU!

Belief #1

It is much easier to be faithful to your future spouse when you realize he/she is not just any person, but God's specific person chosen just for you. I realize that for some hearing this for the very first time the idea that God has a specific person chosen for someone to marry may sound unusual, because it is so **contrary to our culture,** and may take some time to warm-up to. I, myself, didn't come to this conclusion overnight. It was a series of incremental belief changes that led me to this conclusion. But, it was this belief that revolutionized my life as a twenty-four-year-old Christian single by giving me a completely different outlook on male/female relationships, which in turn caused a chain reaction of positive behavior changes. I will be explaining the different merits of this belief throughout various points of this book.

If you study Genesis 2:18-25 you will discover that God's pattern for marriage written there continues to be valid for our lives today. As we begin reading in verse eighteen, pay attention to every place it says **the man** in these verses, *"The LORD God said, 'It is not good for **the man** to be alone. I will make a helper suitable* *for him.' Now the LORD God had formed out of the ground all the beasts of the field and all the birds of the air. He brought them to* **the man** *to see what he would name them; and whatever* **the man** *called each living creature, that was its name. So* **the man** *gave names to all the livestock, the birds of the air and all the beasts of the field. But for Adam no suitable helper was found. So the LORD God caused* **the man** *to fall into a deep sleep; and while he was sleeping, he took one of* **the man's** *ribs and closed up the place with flesh. Then the LORD God made a woman from the rib he had taken out of* **the man**, *and he brought her to* **the man**. **The man** *said, 'This is now bone of my bones and flesh of my flesh; she shall be called "woman," for she was taken out of man.' For this reason* **a man** *will leave his father and mother and be united to his wife, and they will become one flesh"* (emphasis added). Notice in verse twenty-four there is, for the first time, a reference to **a man**. This is significant because previously, in verses eighteen through twenty-three, all the references have been to **the man**, but never **a man**. The phrase **the man** is translated from the Hebrew word 'adam, pronounced (aw-dawm') and by following the context of the use of this phrase we can see that it is referring to Adam. In fact, nine times Adam is referred to in this manner. Now, for the very first time in verse twenty-four, there is a reference to **a man**, translated from the Hebrew word 'iysh pronounced (eesh), so the reference is not referring to Adam. Who, then, is Genesis 2:24 referring to? Since we are told that **a man** should leave his father and mother, it is referring to people who have a father and a mother. Adam couldn't leave his father and mother in view of the fact he was a created being. Adam and Eve didn't have a natural father and mother. They were created by the Father. So, this Scripture is speaking to everyone after them; to those of us who have a human father and mother.

Genesis 2:18-25 begins with a historical account of how the first marriage originated with Adam and Eve, and then it suddenly and unexpectedly switches to a present-day application of that historical account in verse twenty-four. Therefore, we should then pay close attention to their story so we can follow that pattern. God's best for all of us is to follow the pattern He set with Adam and Eve. I refer to this portion of Scripture as God's Marriage Model.

This Marriage Model found in Genesis 2:24 has great significance, as we find it is quoted in two other places in the Bible. Jesus referred to it in Matthew, chapter nineteen, in verses three through five as the answer to a question about divorce. "*Some Pharisees came to him to test him. They asked, 'Is it lawful for a man to divorce his wife for any and every reason?' 'Haven't you read,' he replied,* [Didn't you read the Bible?] '*that at the beginning* [Talking about Genesis] *the Creator "made them male and female,"* [He's referring to Genesis 1:27] *and said, "For this reason a man will leave his father and mother and be united to his wife, and the two will become one flesh?"'*" [Quoting Genesis 2:24] When trying to solve a problem we must first examine what has caused the problem to begin with. That's exactly what Jesus was doing in this instance. Jesus pointed to the root cause of divorce as not following the instructions found here in Genesis. What Jesus was trying to convey here is similar to the old saying: "When all else fails, read the instructions!"

Another present day application of Genesis 2:24 is found in Ephesians, chapter five. Here we find Genesis 2:24 being quoted during information being given to us on how a husband should relate to his wife, which is found in verses twenty-eight through thirty-two. As you can see, God's Marriage Model is vital to our current day events.

A Specific Person

In light of the importance of learning from God's Marriage Model, we should learn about the concept of God having a specific person for someone to marry as found in Genesis 2:21, when reading about Adam and Eve. "*So the LORD God caused the man to fall into a deep sleep; and while he was sleeping, he took one of the man's ribs and closed up the place with flesh.*" Notice that God took only one rib from Adam to make his one mate, thereby indicating just how specific that person really is. He could have easily taken a half-dozen ribs, made a half-dozen women and allowed Adam to pick his favorite. But God didn't do that. It wasn't because it was too much work to make more than one woman, or that He didn't like spare ribs. God didn't create more than one woman for a good reason; His choice fits into His perfect plan.

Please don't use the legalistic view of one rib. What happens if someone's spouse dies? Have they used up their one specific person? No, that would be a legalistic way of thinking! God is more concerned with the reason for the principle than He is the rule created from the principle.

We can further validate the specific person belief if we understand that God has a specific plan for each of our lives. That plan was established for us before we were born. *"__All__ the days ordained for me were written in your book __before__ one of them came to be"* (Psalm 139:16, emphasis added). Prior to your first day of conception, God ordained each of the following days of your life's journey. The Bible also says, *"__Before__ I formed you in the womb I knew you, __before__ you were born I set you apart;"* (Jeremiah 1:5, emphasis added). Before you were born God gave you gifts and talents in order to fulfill His plan and purpose in your life. His plan for your life is what you are called to do. Respecting that plan is a must for those who want to please Him.

The plan God has for your life is very specific. To paraphrase Acts 17:26b, *"God determined the times set for us and the exact places where we should live."* It is no coincidence when and where you were born; God is a specific God. In addition, we find in Ephesians 2:10, *"For we are God's workmanship, created in Christ Jesus **to do good works**, which God prepared **in advance** for us to do"* (emphasis added). We also discover God is even interested in the smallest details in our life, *"The steps of a good man are ordered by the LORD"* (Psalm 37:23 KJV).

Because His plan is so specific, why wouldn't it make sense that it includes the person we should marry? Particularly because this choice has such a major effect on our ability to follow God's plan in other areas of life. Christians seem to have no problem accepting the fact that we do not get to choose our spiritual gifts and callings. That we shouldn't work just anywhere of our choosing or even attend church wherever we want. No, they seek God for guidance in those areas. Yet, when it comes to something even more important, such as choosing a mate, they believe there isn't one specific choice. In the same way as they would seek God in those other issues, they should also seek God when deciding whom to marry. *Therefore*, the *conclusion* for those called to marriage must be that God's specific plan DOES INCLUDE a specific person to marry.

Although most will marry, we should **not assume** it's God's plan for everyone. He does call some to remain single, so we shouldn't pressure those who are called to stay single to get married. Because we don't know which people those are, it is best to not assume it is God's will for any specific individual to get married.

Trust God

Why, then, is it so hard for some people to believe God has created a specific person for them to marry? Usually, it's because they don't trust Him with that choice. They believe they can make a better choice than God. Such arrogance is the basis of all sin. Since God is much wiser than we are, He will always make the better choice. To believe that He wouldn't is to believe He is somehow cruel and wants to punish us with a bad choice. God is not cruel, and He is completely trustworthy, beyond our highest expectations. When a person truly trusts God, they will gladly surrender the choice of whom to marry over to Him.

At the heart of this issue of God having a specific person for someone to marry is *who* does the *choosing* of one's *mate*, God or them? Who really is in *charge*? In today's culture we are so spoiled with the amount of choices we have. If you doubt that, just go to the grocery store and look in the cereal aisle and see how many different types there are to choose from. Promoting any concept that suggests the *limiting* of our options down to *one* is viewed, more often than not, as being a negative, and one that is contrary to our current culture. But that is certainly not true in this case! Nevertheless, we must not *conform* to the society we live in; we must choose to pursue God's will with all of our heart.

Warnings

Let me be quick to point out that the person you are meant to marry is God's best for you, but he/she is not perfect. That's why I refer to them as a specific person, not a perfect person. People sometimes confuse God having a *specific* person for them to marry with Him having a *perfect* person for them to marry. Many people have been disillusioned by this "perfect person" concept and that error has produced disastrous results. That type of thinking leads to other erroneous thought such as, "All I have to do is meet my specific person and there will be nothing to work on, so I can get married the next day." This would be highly improbable because the person God designed for them to marry is not a perfect person, and neither are they.

Knowing who to marry is just the beginning; there is a lot more work ahead in learning how to relate to one another. If you skip the time needed to develop a great relationship prior to marriage, you will set yourselves up for a lot of unnecessary problems. Therefore, the need for marriage preparation is still required. And choosing the specific person doesn't mean there won't be any difficult times once you are married.

We must avoid the trap of thinking that all it takes is marrying God's specific person and from then on there will not be any difficulties. Adam was the first to have such a belief. He thought Eve was perfect because God gave her to him. Remember, everything God had given Adam up to that point was perfect. As a result, he became mad at God and blamed Him for his disobedience, because "the woman" He gave him wasn't perfect.

Another issue that often occurs by believing in the "perfect person" theory arises when a person rejects God's mate choice on the basis of having found an imperfection in the one they thought was supposed to be perfect. Finding imperfections in another person should be *expected* and does not *disqualify* them from being God's chosen person. I am not saying that the other person's shortcomings should be ignored! In fact, there are many character issues that absolutely must be resolved in order to have a good relationship.

CHAPTER 5

BE FAITHFUL
RIGHT NOW!

Belief #2

Knowing God has a specific person for someone to marry means that there is a specific person to be faithful to right now. Just because a person doesn't know who their future spouse is, doesn't mean that person doesn't exist right now, and therefore they cannot be unfaithful to them. The truth is, God's specific person for someone doesn't one day become that person—they were chosen by God before the world began, and *presently* are that specific person. Therefore, as I have already mentioned, having a boyfriend/girlfriend relationship with anyone who is **not** your specific person is being unfaithful to your future spouse. Why? As I already mentioned in chapter one, because you are giving away pieces of your heart by creating memories of emotional and physical attachments. Unfortunately, the memories from those attachments, if not repented of, can afterward be brought into a future marriage as harmful baggage. It is the reliving of those memories after marriage that tramples on the God inspired design of a one man/one woman relationship created for marriage. It is easier to never create those memories in the first place, than it is to forget them.

Whenever a person is **<u>unsure</u>** of whether or not a particular person is their future spouse, a boyfriend/girlfriend relationship would be inappropriate. It is not worth the risk of being unfaithful, or causing someone else to be unfaithful. Always find out first if that person is God's specific choice for you before entering into a relationship with them.

When I use the word *unfaithful* I am using it in its broadest sense, not just a narrow meaning of a certain physical immoral act. Faithfulness to a person does mean to save that one particular physical act for marriage, but that is not all it means. It also includes saving all romantic interest and all of the "firsts" that belong to a future spouse. One way to view this is for a person to see themselves as already married. Would it be acceptable for them as a married person to have a boyfriend/girlfriend, in addition to the person they have married? Should they romantically kiss other people they are not married to? Should they look at people and wonder if that person would be a good person to be married to? These types of thoughts and actions are not appropriate after a person gets married, and neither are they before they do.

I believe the strength of a decision is in the length of that decision. To commit to loving a person for five minutes is easy. To commit to loving a person for the rest of your life, after you have met them, is a strong commitment. But when you commit to loving a person before you meet them and for the rest of your life, you have made the strongest commitment one can make to a relationship. It is a testimony of the degree of commitment you will bring to your future spouse.

When it comes to being faithful to a future spouse, it is harmful to view the boyfriend/girlfriend relationship from a selfish perspective. Using a self-centered perspective causes many of the problems we have in marriages today. It is not what someone should be practicing prior to taking the marriage vows. On the other hand, it is beneficial to view the commitment to that relationship from the other person's perspective. To view this from the other person's perspective, ask yourself some questions similar to those I used in the previous paragraph—"What would I want my future spouse to be doing?

Having other boyfriends/girlfriends? Kissing other people? etc. If that's not what I want my future spouse to be doing, then I shouldn't be doing that either." The idea of viewing our actions through the lens of another person is found in Matthew 7:12 where we read, *"So in everything, do to others what you would have them do to you, for this sums up the Law and the Prophets."*

Once again, let's only concern ourselves with a from now on message, by not condemning ourselves if we have had any past relationships not ordained from God. You can't change the past. You are, however, responsible for your future. The goal is to do our best to arrive at the marriage altar with a whole heart, free of emotional and physical baggage!

CHAPTER 6

FAITHFULNESS BEGINS WITH EMOTIONAL PURITY

Belief #3

Emotional unfaithfulness can be defined as nurturing romantic thoughts and feelings for someone who is not, nor ever will be, your spouse. It is the "Special" attention given to someone. While it is normal for single men and women to be tempted with romantic thoughts and feelings for someone, it is harmful for them to entertain or act on those desires and feelings by giving their heart to different people. Just as it is harmful for a married person to give his or her heart to someone they are not married to, a single person needs to **practice** what is required in marriage—Faithfulness. All of those romantic feelings are best saved for a future spouse.

Defining Emotions

Before I can continue any further, I must address a common issue so I do not lose some of the men that are reading this. Some guys are actually insulted when I tell them that emotional purity applies to them. They become insulted because they consider themselves to not be emotional and are proud of that. Such men incorrectly believe that emotions consist only of crying and group hugs. While those responses are certainly a show of emotion, there is a whole range of items that fit into the category of emotions besides that. While males may not typically major in the same emotions as females, they still experience a range of emotions.

It is important to realize that emotions are just feelings, both good and bad, and we all have them. Feelings come as a response to what we are thinking about. Pleasure, anger, joy, courage, lust, accomplishment and loneliness are **all** feelings. An exuberant outburst for that winning touchdown is a show of emotion. Oh, and by the way, for the guys that are proud of not having emotions, pride is an emotion! So, for those of you men who believe that emotional purity doesn't apply to you, think again!

Some people believe that as long as they haven't actually crossed the physical boundaries that God created for romantic expressions, then they have not sinned. They do not consider it a sin if he or she is only thinking thoughts about inappropriately crossing the physical boundary. But the truth is, as far as sin goes, there isn't any difference between thinking on those wrong thoughts than there is in acting on them. It really does matter what we are thinking about. Jesus shares that thought in Matthew 5:27-28 when He said, *"You have heard that it was said, 'Do not commit adultery.' But I tell you that anyone who **looks** at a woman lustfully has **already** committed **adultery** with her in his heart"* (emphasis added). Jesus is telling us that a person being lustful has <u>already</u> committed adultery, even though nothing physical ever happened. Sin always begins with a thought before it progresses into an action (James 1:14-15). Therefore, we must guard our heart to keep our thoughts and emotions pure, in order to keep our actions pure.

If we merely attempt to adhere to the boundaries concerning immoral physical acts and not stay within those created for emotional involvement, once the emotional boundaries are crossed, the physical boundaries will likely follow. *Physical purity always starts with emotional purity*. If a person never violates the emotional boundary of purity, he or she will never violate the physical boundary. Therefore, if a person never **imagines**, **fantasizes**, or even **hopes** for the opportunity to do something immoral, they will never do it. It is the entertaining of such thoughts that makes immoral actions possible.

It is unwise to think we could use any part of our being in a way that is intended for marriage, without producing a subsequent physical response that is also only intended for marriage. Your body has no idea whether you're married or not. God didn't create different bodies, one for singles and one for married folks. If anyone gives their body romantic input, emotional or physical, they should expect that it will want to respond to that input! God made our bodies to respond that way.

The majority of churches today do not condone immoral physical acts, but flirting among those who are not married is generally viewed as innocent, **because** it is typically done in a playful way and is often thought of as harmless fun. I disagree! If we examine *why* a person flirts with another, we will see that it is anything but above reproach. Flirting is an act that is used to tease another person in order to create an emotional response which is reserved for marriage. Therefore, it is wrong to do that outside of marriage, or for a married person to do so with someone they are not married to. One problem with provoking an emotional response with someone a person is not, nor will ever be married to, is that it is being emotionally unfaithful by not saving all of a person's emotion for their marriage partner. We have giggled and winked at this immoral practice for too long. It is against God's standard.

Flirting is many times used in a way that is similar to fishing, whereby a person throws out a comment in an attempt to see if its recipient will take the bait by accepting that remark. If the comment is accepted, then they know that the other person is romantically interested in them. If not, then they aren't. The hope is that a repeated volley can take place to create an emotional fantasy in the other person, with the person doing the flirting being the object of that fantasy. The most common reason people flirt with one another is to create that emotional response, hoping it will later turn into a physical response.

Being emotionally faithful also includes staying away from nurturing romantic thoughts about celebrities such as actors, actresses, sports figures, etc. Although it is popular in our society today for people to become infatuated with such people, they should not be worshiped or idolized. People often let their guard down from considering such celebrities to be a person he or she can be emotionally unfaithful with, because they don't actually know them, or in most probability will never meet them. But, we must never consider them to be exempt from being someone a person can be unfaithful with, because to be truly faithful there can't be **any** exceptions.

Social Media

In the electronic age that we now live in, there are different methods of communication that people engage in that are not inherently bad, but that can be used in a harmful way. Social Media, for example, has made it easier for people to become emotionally involved with one another. People are communicating in a way that they never would if they were face to face, or even conversing by telephone. Private information that is not meant to be shared with just anyone is now casually shared with only acquaintances, or worse, strangers. Unfortunately, this type of communication allows a person to become overly familiar with another by granting them access into their private life. We must, therefore, cautiously proceed when using this form of communication.

Flirting via Social Media has been made easier because people are more willing to take unnatural risks that cross emotional boundaries. Inappropriate behavior is now performed from a safe distance, under the cloak of privacy, making it less intimidating for someone to expose themselves openly to humiliation and rejection. For whatever reason, some people lose touch with reality when using forms of electronic communications. Maybe it's the result of indirect human interaction that has convinced them they are isolated from the rejection and disgust of unwelcomed comments, I am not sure. However, I do know that the content of this type of communication has gotten way out of hand.

It used to be that people would pass flirtatious notes in class and, unlike Social Media, they were able to immediately see the reaction of the person who received that note to determine if the advance was welcomed. I am not saying that any method of flirting to create an ungodly desire in someone is ever acceptable, because it is not. I am just contrasting the two different methods.

The frequency in which people communicate through Social Media and texting has risen to unbelievable heights. The problem with this continual communication is that it forces two people to think about each other often and over a long period of time. This type of constant communication soon becomes the equivalent of spending enormous amounts of private time with the other person. In some ways, it's not much different than if two people spent time alone.

Would a loving father allow his fourteen-year-old daughter to spend an entire day home alone with a seventeen-year-old young man with ungodly values? No! People would be up in arms, crying child abuse. And yet, some of those same people wouldn't think twice about that same scenario if it had taken place over the Internet, with the same two people constantly communicating back and forth throughout the day. Why? It seems that some parents are only interested in protecting their children from immoral **physical** activity and not from immoral **emotional** activity. The truth is, as parents, we are the protectors of our children both emotionally and physically. We should monitor our child's electronic interaction with the same scrutiny we would use to monitor where they go for their activities.

One possible result of this type of attention grabbing through constant contact can be the inadvertent or intentional romantic desires that are created for someone. We must realize that God created us in such a way that whatever we give our time and attention to we will have a desire for. He intended us to use that for good, but it is not always used that way. Whenever a person gives time and attention to someone else, the possibility exists to create bonds, desires, and feelings that should never have been created. I am not saying that it always results in creating romantic desires, but the risk is there. There isn't an exact formula that can determine when a person's constant contact will turn into a romantic desire, so it is up to us to be on guard to prevent it. It is, however, a recipe for disaster when a person combines the constant contact with inappropriate content.

Parents are responsible for protecting their children from allowing their emotions to go unchecked, but ultimately that responsibility must also get passed down to their children. Everyone should be on guard against allowing their own emotions to run wild. Parents should train their children in this principle when they are younger, but, as they grow older, it then also becomes the child's responsibility to guard his or her own heart. It is up to every individual to see the danger in such activity and not allow it to harm them or anyone else.

Motive

Because it takes on so many forms, it is impossible to cover every way a person can be emotionally unfaithful. I cannot provide you with a complete list of actions to avoid, since it is not the actions by themselves that make the behavior harmful—it is the hidden motive behind it. This is a **heart issue.** It will require more effort and brutal honesty to discover the true motive behind the actions. When attempting to determine if an action is inappropriate or not, the principle to remember is: **Anytime a person willingly allows their emotions to cross the brother/sister boundary with someone who is not their future spouse, he or she is being unfaithful.** No one ever benefits from that type of behavior.

Handling Temptation

Resisting a temptation is a very good thing to practice. It is like building a muscle in that it increases with use. Every person must learn how to deal with temptations that come to them without their control. Even though a person may be tempted, he/she doesn't have to act on or dwell on that temptation for any length of time. Regardless of how small a time dwelling on it may be, an immediate rejection of a temptation always works the best. We become more vulnerable to that specific temptation if we have previously given in to it. The frequency of that temptation also increases if that temptation is not resisted. Once a temptation is welcomed into our lives, we are guaranteed it will bring its friends.

A fine example of being able to resist temptation is found in Genesis 39:7-20, the story of Joseph and Potiphar's wife. Joseph was being seduced by Potiphar's wife to secretly commit an immoral act with her. There were additionally tempting circumstances in this situation because of Potiphar being away. Joseph could have easily rationalized this act by thinking, "No one will ever know, so what harm could it do?" The fact that Joseph had the inclination to run from that situation tells me that he beforehand had practiced resisting temptation. He spent no time at all debating within himself his course of action; his decision was based on a predetermined and practiced set of beliefs. His resistance to that temptation hadn't been weakened by previous failure of giving in to the "lesser" temptation of privately entertaining lustful thoughts.

It is possible to determine the grip that immorality has on you, particularly with men. In today's society we are constantly being bombarded with immoral images, but it is how we handle that temptation that will determine its influence upon us. Test yourself by measuring the amount of reaction time it takes to turn away from an immoral temptation when you are presented with it. The slower the reaction time indicates a greater hold that immorality has on you, while a faster reaction time means exactly the opposite.

I need to clarify that the brief temptation of immoral thoughts by itself should not be considered sin. There are some thoughts that pursue us without our permission. Those unwanted thoughts are not sin unless we welcome them and take them in as our own. In that case such thoughts are only temptations. We are told in 2 Corinthians 10:5 (KJV) what we should do with those temptations. It is exactly the same thing we should do with any other immoral thought: "*Casting down imaginations, and every high thing that exalteth itself against the knowledge of God, and bringing into **captivity** every thought to the obedience of Christ*" (emphasis added). Those thoughts that are not welcome guests need to be taken captive. If they are not imprisoned, those thoughts will captivate us, meaning we will be imprisoned. One way or another, someone or something will be imprisoned. It is our choice as to who or what it will be.

Avoiding a Broken Heart

Remaining emotionally pure is beneficial to a person, because it helps them avoid ever having a broken heart over a failed relationship not of God. What is a broken heart? It is pain caused by doing something you shouldn't have done. It is similar to putting your hand on a hot stove. When you do that, it produces pain. The pain lets you know you are hurting yourself and you should remove your hand immediately from the stove. The pain comes even if you touched the stove accidentally. Pain isn't concerned with our motives, it is sent to protect us, regardless of our intentions. It teaches us it would be wise to not do that again.

All too often, people ignore that warning from the pain caused by a broken heart. Instead, they indiscriminately get into another romantic relationship to try to cover the pain of the last broken relationship with the excitement of a new one. This repeated cycle only serves to make matters worse by compounding the problem with yet another broken heart. Tragically, this flawed solution, regardless of how many times it is applied, never solves the original problem of the heartbreak caused by entering into a relationship not ordained of God.

It was never God's intent that a person should ever have a broken heart over a romantic relationship. He never designed or intended us to have more than one romantic relationship in our lifetime, let alone a series of intimate relationships, either emotionally or physically. He intentionally created us this way for a reason. He wanted our very first romantic relationship to last a lifetime. That's why a broken heart is devastating, it's because romantic attachments were meant to be permanent. That's also why a person should *only* begin a romantic relationship with their specific person so that relationship can last a lifetime.

Of course, there are some exceptions to this, such as the death of a spouse, for example. I also realize people make mistakes in the area, so I am not saying this to condemn people but to explain a benefit God has for us.

When possible it is best to have only one romantic relationship. But, for those of you who have already been involved in a relationship not ordained by God, let me again say to you, God's best for you is to acknowledge that relationship as being wrong, even if you didn't know at the time it was wrong. Then commit from this point forward to have only one romantic relationship. Never should anyone think, "I have already messed up, so what does it really matter if I do the wrong thing again?" With each mistake we make, there is more damage done. Always limit your mistakes. Make the best of whatever situation you find yourself in.

CHAPTER 7

RELATIONSHIP BOUNDARIES

Belief #4

We need to learn how to have biblical relationships with all members of the opposite gender and must maintain them throughout our entire life. Those who are not yet married must treat all of the opposite gender as a natural brother or sister to guard against being unfaithful to his or her future spouse. 1 Timothy 5:1b-2 tells us to, *"Treat younger men as brothers, older women as mothers, and younger women as sisters, with absolute purity."* The Phillips translation puts it this way: *"Treat them as younger sisters with purity and no more."* True brother/sister relationships are dedicated to the spiritual and physical well-being of the other person. This would include treating all members of the opposite gender as a natural brother or sister, not only physically, but also emotionally.

A true brother or sister would not exploit a relationship with any member of the opposite gender by seeing them as a form of entertainment, or as a pool of potential mates to sort through. Neither person should use the other for selfish gain. Lust is a selfish motive that harms relationships. Lust is a desire for inappropriate physical or emotional pleasure. It is not at all the same as love; in fact, it is the exact opposite. A genuine brother/sister relationship should, instead, inspire each person in it to grow closer to God and not distract them from that relationship.

If a person only relates to members of the opposite gender in a flirting manner or as a perspective marriage partner, what happens when they get married? Do they automatically change? If a person doesn't learn while he or she is single how to treat the opposite gender as a brother/sister, this could lead to problems after marriage. It takes practice to learn how to have godly opposite gender relationships.

Young men need to be trained early on to love as Christ loves. They need to understand they are to protect women, rather than selfishly using them for their own lustful pleasure. Job 31:1 admonishes men this way: "*I made a covenant with my eyes not to look lustfully at a girl.*" Males of any age should not encourage females to dress in an immoral manner. We were made to be protectors, not consumers! All too often, we see young men rewarding scantily dressed young women with special attention. Instead the protector within those men should rise up and want to protect those women from the danger that type of immodesty can attract. They should take on the responsibility to protect them from the predators that come to prey upon such young women during this vulnerable time and encourage their modesty.

Relationship Boundaries

God purposely placed a boundary between brother/sister relationships and marriage relationships. He did this to separate the two types of relationships in order to make the marriage relationship unique. It is the blurring of this line that has caused many of the relationship problems we see today. One of the problems that can occur is the defrauding of another individual. We are told in the King James Version of 1 Thessalonians 4:6a in reference to protecting marriage, "*That no man go beyond and defraud his brother in any matter*" (emphasis added). The word *brother* here refers to mankind, not just males. The phrase "go beyond" refers to overstepping a boundary. Once a person has purposely entertained romantic thoughts and feelings for someone he/she will never marry, that person has overstepped the brother/sister boundary by doing something that only belongs in a marriage relationship. When this happens, a person is now in danger of defrauding someone.

God then lets us know in the second part of verse six and continuing in verse seven, how serious He is about people not crossing this boundary line and defrauding someone. *"That no man **go beyond** and **defraud** his brother in any matter: because that the Lord is the __avenger__ of all such, as we also have __forewarned__ you and testified"* (KJV, emphasis added). *⁷ For God did not call us to be impure, but to live a holy life.* Since this is such a serious issue, we should investigate further what defrauding is, to effectively avoid this type of destructive relationship.

Commitment to Marriage

*Defrauding in a relationship takes place when a person forms a relationship that crosses the brother/sister boundary, thus **implying** a lifelong commitment to marriage, only to later back out of that commitment.* We must be painfully aware of this fact, because not every person who crosses the brother/sister boundary does so with the intent of entering a lifelong commitment to the other person. However, entering into that type of relationship **implies** that commitment, regardless if that was the intention or not. Unfortunately, in today's culture, most boyfriend/girlfriend relationships are typically not committed relationships; they are usually formed from the onset with the intentions of being temporary.

Even if someone would attempt to make that type of relationship temporary, they will ultimately fail at that attempt. It is impossible to separate the treating of someone as *more* than a brother or sister from making a lifetime commitment to them. It is like going swimming and not getting wet—it simply cannot be done. The only reason a person should cross the brother/sister boundary is for the lifelong commitment of marriage.

I once saw an ad on a bulletin board that read: "Wedding dress for sale—never used." I couldn't help but think that, although the dress was never used, the affections of the bride-to-be were. A relationship someone had promised would last forever was now over. All of the expectations of being married to that individual were now gone. This bride-to-be was defrauded.

Stealing a Gift

To gain a better understanding of how a person can be defrauded in a relationship, we need to define the term. The word defraud has an interesting connotation. It means to cheat out of, scam, deceive, use trickery, swindle, dupe, pose as an impostor, or misrepresent. It is much *different* than stealing from someone without their knowledge, such as a thief in the night would do. To defraud someone implies that the deceiver has fraudulently gained *consent*, in the sense that there must be a *willing* party. But just because someone *willingly* allows another person to steal from them does not make the theft right.

What is being stolen when someone defrauds another are the emotions and affections that are intended to be an exclusive gift belonging only to that person's future spouse! That gift is the gift of "firsts"—the first person they have ever had romantic feelings for, the first person they have ever kissed, held hands with, etc. Everyone who will eventually marry has been made a trustee of this gift for their future spouse. When someone allows another to defraud them of the gift, he/she is giving away something that should have been saved for their mate. They are allowing their gift of the exclusiveness of their romantic emotions and affections to their future spouse to be stolen and squandered on someone to whom it doesn't belong.

Defrauding is an inconsiderate act of selfishness. It is outright thievery to enter into a relationship with someone to gratify oneself with the emotions and affections of another person that belong to someone else. Why would anyone want to steal this precious gift from another? Such a tragic violation of an awesome gift! No person should want to have these gifts stolen from them, nor should they be willing to steal them from someone else. Stealing from one's spiritual brother or sister is even worse. On the other hand, *being faithful to their future spouse preserves that gift, and keeps them from defrauding anyone.*

Repeated Qualifier

What I have just stated about the gift of "firsts" is the ideal, but we must always realize that God is able to work with less than the ideal. In fact, that's what He specializes in! So to make absolutely sure this truth is not misunderstood, I will repeat what I have stated earlier, so that no one feels hopeless or condemned. For anyone who has **already** been involved in a relationship not ordained by God, God's best for them is to acknowledge that relationship as being harmful to a future marriage, even if they didn't know at the time it was wrong. Then commit from this point forward to have only one romantic relationship. Don't add to that mistake by condemning yourself. That won't help! Not only is it impossible to change the past, it's foolish to try. You are, however, responsible for your future. *Never* should anyone think, "I have already messed up, so what does it really matter if I do the wrong thing again?" With each mistake we make there is more damage done. Always limit your mistakes and make the best of whatever situation you find yourself in. We must approach this from the approach Jesus proclaimed: "Go and sin no more." It's never too late to commit to be faithful from now on!

Defrauding Takes Two

If we understand *when* defrauding first begins to take place, we can better avoid it. As we have already read in 1 Thessalonians 4:6, crossing the brother/sister boundary can lead to the defrauding of another person. But this does not mean that *every time* a person crosses that boundary without a lifelong commitment to marriage, they have defrauded someone. There is more to defrauding than that.

Defrauding is not something a person can do alone; it can only happen *after* **two** people form a mutual relationship. Keep in mind that not every time a person inappropriately crosses the brother/sister boundary, he or she does it **along with** someone else. A person can cross that boundary all by themselves when they allow their thoughts and emotions to drift into territory that is reserved specifically for marriage, and this can be done *without* the aid or cooperation of another person. In fact, the person they are having those feelings for may not have a clue that it is happening. Under those circumstances there isn't any defrauding taking place. In order to defraud someone there must be consent, regardless of how ill-advised that consent may be. Without the consent of *both* parties, defrauding cannot take place. Defrauding actually begins the moment two willing parties involve themselves in a *temporary* relationship that crosses the brother/sister boundary.

Please don't misunderstand me! I am not saying there isn't anything wrong with inappropriately crossing the boundary as long as there isn't any defrauding. Crossing that line for any other reason but for marriage is still wrong. Because the person he/she would be entertaining these feelings for is not their future spouse, it would mean they are being unfaithful to their future spouse. That concept remains true. I am merely trying to point out the moment at which defrauding begins. I'm not trying to justify wrong actions.

We must be careful to not fall into the temptation of blaming only the person doing the deceiving at this point. Actually, both parties have done something wrong in this situation—one has created an illusion, the other has believed it. The deceiver has done something much worse in this case, but that doesn't mean that the one who has believed that deceiver is completely void of responsibility. We all have a responsibility for what we believe, therefore all of the blame doesn't solely fall on the deceiver. A person can never be truly set free from the hurt and harm a deceiver has brought upon them, without first accepting the responsibility of having allowed them to do so. That may be hard to do, but it is necessary!

Multiple Thefts

Since defrauding requires two people to be involved with each other, there are multiple thefts that come as a result. I will illustrate this by using a fictitious story. Let's say God intends for two couples, John and Jane to one day marry each other, likewise with Marty and Mary. At this point in John's life he has no idea that God wants him to marry Jane. John's eyes begin to wander and he decides that Mary is someone he is attracted to. So, John then begins to flatter Mary with kind words and special attention in order to stir up romantic emotions within Mary toward him. If John is successful in gaining the emotions and affections of Mary, he then becomes an accomplice in cheating Marty—Mary's future spouse—out of the blessings that can only be bestowed if Mary would have saved all of her emotions and affections for him. John has stolen from Mary what belongs to Marty.

If that wasn't bad enough, John had to cross the brother/sister line when he enticed and encouraged Mary to give her emotions and affections to him. In order to enter into a relationship with Mary, John had to bait Mary by spending his emotions and affections on her, and in doing so has now created memories and emotional attachments with her. Therefore, John also didn't protect his gift of "firsts" for Jane, and has cheated Jane out of receiving all of John's romantic emotions and affections. Since Mary helped to facilitate John's misconduct, she has stolen from Jane. We can now see how one unbiblical relationship will hurt a *minimum* of four people.

After a brief relationship with Mary, John comes to the realization that he has done the wrong thing. He knows he is being unfaithful to his future spouse and that he has to end his relationship with Mary to make it right. John asks God and Mary to forgive him. He then decides that from that point on he will enter into only one romantic relationship and that will be with his future spouse. Once John eventually meets Jane, he will then also ask her to forgive him for not following God's perfect plan and for the harm he has caused her.

True Love Honors the Boundaries

Often people, under the guise of "love," involve themselves in relationships they should never be in. Even if someone's emotions have them convinced they are in love, that doesn't mean they are. Emotions are unreliable! If it is someone's intent to show love to another person who they know is not their specific person, or are unsure if they are, then crossing the boundary of a brother/sister relationship and having a boyfriend/girlfriend relationship with them is a terrible way to show love. If they really loved that person, they wouldn't want to cause them to be unfaithful to their future spouse. It is therefore unbiblical, and consequently unloving, to treat a person in a way that would gain his/her romantic affections while knowing there is even the slightest possibility that you would consider backing out of the relationship. Accepting another person's romantic affections is only allowable if you know there will be a lifetime marriage covenant between the two of you. Real love considers the preciousness of others and would **restrain** them from going beyond a true friendship under these circumstances. *True love honors the boundaries God has placed between brother/sister relationships and marriage relationships.*

The only person from whom you should receive romantic emotions and affections is the person who will be, or who already is your spouse. All others should be kindly rejected. As for someone who isn't yet your spouse, but someday will be, the affections received from them should only be of a non-physical nature. Those affections must be placed on hold until after the wedding.

Self-Esteem

A real temptation that many will face is being pressured to think he or she needs a boyfriend/girlfriend to be complete. Supposedly, they have to date to be special. As a result, many unwisely rest all of their hopes of building self-esteem on acquiring their "trophy" date. It is harmful to place all hopes of happiness into the care of any one person. When someone has unrealistic expectations of that person being their ultimate source for happiness, they have placed a burden upon him or her that can in no way be fulfilled by them. The danger is great when you allow any one individual to become your #1 priority. Save yourself from that danger by choosing to practice what is required in marriage now! Make God #1; your spouse will be #2. This is the best way to love them.

Making God a higher priority is vital because it is from that relationship with God that one is given the ability and the incentive to do all of what we have been discussing. It is from that relationship with God and our desire to serve Him that one develops the maturity and preparation needed for marriage.

In order to be content, we should be receiving our identity from God and having our need for love met by Him. People who do not have their love need met by God are truly needy people. Needy people are discontented and, sadly, that discontent drives other people away. Real self-esteem doesn't come from what other people think about you. If you think it does, you'd better hold on and be prepared for an emotional roller coaster ride. People will like you one day, but not the next. On the other hand, perfect self-esteem is independent of popular opinion. Don't make the mistake of putting a high priority on trying to fit in. Instead, you should learn to stand alone with God as your sole supporter. Real self-esteem comes from knowing what God thinks about you, and what He thinks never changes.

Your relationship with God is crucial to having successful relationships with others. **You will never have a better relationship with any person than the level of relationship you have with the Lord.** Let's say your relationship with God is a nine, then there is no way you can have a better relationship with any other person that's higher than an eight. If your relationship with God is a two, you can't have a better relationship with anyone else other than a one! It is through our relationship with Him that we are enabled to love others. That makes perfect sense, because God is love. Besides, if you can't have a great relationship with God, who is perfect, don't fool yourself into thinking you can have a great relationship with someone who is not perfect!

CHAPTER 8

TWO PARALLEL PATHS

What I am about to cover in **Beliefs #5 and #6** demonstrates how God expects us to honor marriage by adhering to its boundaries. To respect marriage, everyone needs to know how to appropriately cross the boundaries of a brother/sister relationship with the person he/she will eventually marry, so they can begin a relationship that will lead to marriage. They also need to know how to not cross the boundaries of a brother/sister relationship inappropriately with the rest of the opposite gender, those whom they will never marry. In our current culture individuals inappropriately cross that boundary, not just once, but often several times. People go back and forth over the line, in and out of the type of relationship that should be reserved only for marriage.

Unfortunately, when a person believes he/she is responsible for searching after and choosing their mate, that person is, at a minimum, bound to cross the brother/sister boundary emotionally, if not eventually physically, with one or more people whom they will never marry. Although it is common today and is incorrectly considered by many to not be harmful, those boundaries are crossed when a person practices romance, or sorts through, compares, and considers their brothers/sisters as potential candidates for marriage.

Such behaviors would not be beneficial in marriage; therefore, they should not be practiced prior to it.

To keep from inappropriately crossing the brother/sister boundary, a person must first believe God has a specific person He has **already chosen** to be their mate, as I have covered earlier. If a person doesn't have to choose because they believe God has already made that choice for them, then there isn't the need to go shopping to make a selection from a group of people. This, in turn, will keep them from violating brother/sister relationships. Of course, this then opens up a new set of questions, such as: How does someone find their specific person, and how do they recognize who that person is? **Beliefs #5 and #6** show us how this is possible.

Belief #5

It is God's responsibility to bring two people together. We can find this in Genesis 2:22 where God brings Eve to Adam. *"Then the LORD God made a woman from the rib he had taken out of the man, and he **brought** her to the man"* (emphasis added). After God puts Adam to sleep and takes one of his ribs, He forms Eve from that rib and then brings Eve back to Adam. This indicates to us that He hadn't formed Eve in Adam's presence, and that by bringing Eve to Adam, God didn't make him search for his mate. People need to trust God to take care of bringing them and their mate together. Discovering your specific person is an event only God should arrange. The best comment I have ever heard regarding this is, "You're not responsible for finding your mate, just for recognizing who they are."

The question becomes, How does someone meet the person they will eventually marry if they don't search for them? The answer: By following God's plan for their life. It doesn't matter if that specific person is on the other side of the world. When both persons involved follow God's plan, their paths will eventually bring them together to walk side by side, to be at the *same place* at the *same time* over a period of time. The time period will be long enough to make their discovery along the way of who their mate is. Maybe the couple will be doing the same type of ministry together as an example.

Picture this as looking like two parallel paths. It is not, as some people incorrectly imagine, an intersection where two people have to be at the same place at the same time in a brief moment in time or they will miss each other forever. With God saying, "Oh, well, sorry you missed your chance." He isn't purposely trying to make this difficult, as some incorrectly believe.

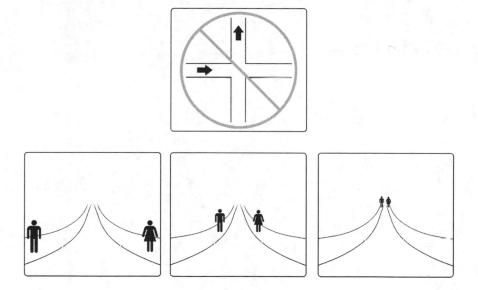

With the Parallel Paths Plan, the discovery doesn't necessarily have to take place right away. A couple may know each other for a period of time without a clue that God is going to eventually reveal to them that they are each other's spouse. Doing it this way gives two people a chance to get to know each other as friends, apart from any romantic interest and the temptation to put on false fronts to impress each other. Since friendship is a great foundation for marriage, this becomes another way of preventing divorce.

CHAPTER 9

GOD WILL LET YOU KNOW

Belief #6

God reveals to a person who the specific person is he or she is to marry. To understand how we find out who it is we are to marry, we must look once again to the pattern God set for us in Genesis, chapter two. We must now ask the question, How did Adam know that Eve was supposed to be his wife? In Genesis 2:21-23 God reveals to Adam who he is to marry. *"So the LORD God caused **the man** to fall into a deep sleep; and while he was sleeping, he took <u>one</u> of **the man's** ribs and closed up the place with flesh. Then the LORD God made a woman from the rib he had taken out of **the man**, and he **brought her** to **the man**"* (emphasis added). After God puts Adam to sleep and takes **one** of his ribs, He then forms Eve from that rib. God then brought Eve to Adam, which indicated that He hadn't formed Eve in Adam's presence. Immediately, Adam recognizes her as his rib when he says in verse twenty-three, *"This is now bone of my bones and flesh of my flesh; she shall be called 'woman,' for she was **taken out of man**"* (emphasis added). In other words, Adam's first response to seeing Eve was, "Hey, this is the rib that was taken out of me." That's what a rib is, flesh and bone.

Adam's first response wasn't to evaluate Eve to see if she was his type or if he liked her or not. Adam's response was to **who** Eve was in **relationship** to him; not any attribute about her. No, this goes beyond any likes or dislikes of a person. Her relationship to him was she was flesh of **his** flesh and bones of **his** bones. This is what sets Eve apart from all of creation. She was the only living being created from Adam's rib. Every living creation at that point other than Eve was made from the dust of the earth.

Remember I quoted earlier, "You're not responsible for finding your mate, just for recognizing who they are." Adam did this when he recognized Eve by referring to her as bone of his bones and flesh of his flesh.

The question then arises, how did he know **she** was his rib? First of all, how did Adam know he was missing a rib? Adam was sleeping when God took his rib. Secondly, why did Adam think she was that rib? She didn't look anything like a rib. He wasn't there when God formed her. Therefore, God was the only person who knew. As far as we know, God didn't introduce Eve as Adam's rib. So, the only way for Adam to know Eve was his rib was for God to reveal that information internally to him. God revealed that Eve was part of Adam, just as God still reveals to people today who their mate is.

Unfortunately, today we see people getting married for all sorts of reasons. "I had this feeling that just wouldn't go away." "She was so attractive." "He made me feel special." However, these are all secondary to the biblical reason found in Genesis 2:18-23. According to Genesis 2:24 there is one specific reason that should lead a person to decide to get married. "***For this reason** a man will leave his father and mother and be united to his wife, and they will become one flesh*" (emphasis added). The subject of verse twenty-four is present day marriages, as we already discussed in the beginning of chapter four. It is interesting to see that verse twenty-four begins with the phrase "For this reason." So we must ask ourselves, what reason is this verse talking about? The phrase "For this reason" is a cause and effect conjunction, indicating there is a link between what has just happened in the previous verses and the subject of marriage which is now being discussed. We can, therefore, find out what that God-ordained reason for marriage is by reading the previous verses leading up to this one. God wants us to make the connection between the reason Adam and Eve got married, which is the pattern, and the reason people should currently get married. The reason Adam married Eve was because he had a revelation of who his mate was. So, for the same reason, we should marry out of revelation, not just feelings. Therefore, the reason someone should get married is because God has revealed to them a specific person to marry. This should be the basis for deciding to marry.

How exactly does God reveal to someone today who the specific person is they are to marry? He knows who it is, but how is He going to communicate that information to us? One frequent way that God reveals to someone who their specific person is takes place by Him giving them His desires. The basis for this is found in Psalm 37:4, *"Delight yourself in the LORD and he will give you the desires of your heart."* This verse does not mean that God will give us whatever we want. But if we are delighting in Him, He will give us **what** we should desire and in the case of marriage, **whom** we should desire. When this happens, a person will one day discover a desire within themselves that wasn't there before and that they didn't create themselves. Furthermore, they are certain that it was God who placed it there.

John 15:7 (RSV) shares with us a truth that is similar to that which is found in Psalm 37:4, Jesus said, *"If you abide in me, and my words abide in you, ask whatever you will, and it shall be done for you."* Again, this is not saying that God will give us whatever we want. It is saying that if we abide in Jesus and His words abide in us, we would never ask for just anything. We would only ask for those things God would want us to ask for.

The prerequisite for receiving God's desires is delighting in Him, as mentioned in Psalm 37:4. Delighting in God is not just thinking He exists. Delighting in Him means you are consumed day and night with thoughts about Him. He is the most exciting part of your life. You are excited about the life He has planned for you because you are certain He is a good God. Therefore, your desire is to follow after what is written in the Bible with all of your heart. Under those conditions, He then will be able to *transfer* His desires over to you.

Receiving this desire for a specific person someone is to marry happens by God putting a desire in them for that specific person. It doesn't happen by them indiscriminately telling God, "I want this person, could you please put the two of us together?" That will create desires, not receive them.

Some people miss the simplicity of receiving revelation from God through our desires because they are looking for something different. They think God **only** works through the dramatic and spectacular, but He is never limited to that. He doesn't have to audibly tell someone or write the message in the sky. Please, don't make this more complicated than it is.

The desire that God gives someone is similar to other desires. The urge to indulge in ice cream is a desire. But the difference between the desires God gives and the desire for ice cream lies in where it came from. One desire comes from seeing a Dairy Queen; the other comes from God.

I want to stress the point of God giving you a desire. We are not to expect God to give us that desire before He decides it is time for us to have it; we must allow God to freely give that to us **at the time He decides to**. That desire given by Him is not something we have control over, so when that is to take place is completely up to Him! This is not something we should allow our own personal expectations to try and control. People get themselves into trouble when **they** decide they want to be married by a certain age.

Warning: We can create our own desires apart from God. A person can create desires by giving someone or something enough time and attention. Therefore, it becomes important to be able to distinguish between our self-created desires and God-sent desires. We can create desire by giving someone or something **enough** positive time and attention. In theory, you can "fall in love" with a fence post, if you give it enough time and attention!

Since it is possible to create your own desires, it is essential to take precautions to stay away from outside influences that would create a desire apart from God in the area of choosing a mate. It takes physical and emotional purity to accurately receive God's desires, and not create a desire for someone that is apart from God's plan. Physical and emotional promiscuity are major factors in creating your own desires.

At this time, please allow me to repeat what I already mentioned in chapter six concerning the dangers of the misuse of Social Media. Due to the frequency in which people communicate through ways such as texting or other Social Media, a person can create a desire for someone by spending too much time communicating with them. This, in turn, provides the opportunity to create bonds and desires that wouldn't otherwise have taken place between people that it shouldn't have.

Sadly, people sometimes take their self-created desires to do what is wrong and blame God for that desire by saying, "I have this desire and it won't go away; it must be God who gave that desire to me." They do not realize they were the ones who created that desire in the first place. God is not at fault in this scenario. Our self-created desires become idols if we are unwilling to surrender all of our desires, hopes, and dreams and lay them at His altar.

Hearing from God

Let me also be quick to point out that it is easy to make a mistake in believing whether you have heard from God or not. Deciding you have heard from God concerning your specific person should be done *soberly*. This cannot be a *hasty* or *emotionally* based decision. Time is your friend, not your enemy. After all, the first thing mentioned about love in 1 Corinthians 13:4 is that love is patient. It is best to examine this information and to put it *thoroughly* to the *test*. Make *absolutely* sure the revelation is *truly* from God before taking any *action* on it. If a person has not already spent time hearing from God on lesser issues, chances are it will be very difficult to hear from Him on this major issue.

We can also lose our sensitivity to God's leading if we spend time in media that proclaims an opposite message. Regardless of what form it takes—movies, songs, or books—any competing message can desensitize us to hearing God's voice. If we willingly allow a portrayal of an opposite standard to entertain us, we are coming into agreement with that standard.

Knowing God has a specific person for marriage may create curiosity as to whom that person will be. It is normal to be tempted to question if this person is the one, or is that person the one. But, as tempting as it may be, don't try to guess! A person has no control over **when** God lets them know. Guessing will lead to creating your own desires apart from God! Guessing crosses over into searching, by continually asking, "Is this the one, or, is that the one?" Not being willing to wait for God's direction in this area leads to torment, constant looking and wondering rather than resting. Isaiah 26:3 (NKJV) states it very well, *"You will keep him in perfect peace, Whose mind is stayed on You, Because he trusts in You."*

Trusting God plays a major factor in keeping us from guessing. Waiting on God's timing is just as much a part of trusting as it is to desire only the person God has for you. True trust is more of a going to sleep to our desire of one day being married through our own ability to make that happen, instead, we should trust that God will do that for us. It is the confidence of knowing one day God will wake us up to the fact of who our specific person is. Until then a person should just go about His business. This is what happened to me. I was serving God, content with being single, when all of a sudden I knew that Lisa would one day be my wife. I was caught totally by surprise. I wasn't thinking about it at all, the timing of the revelation happened unexpectedly in a twinkling of an eye.

When it is interpreted correctly, Proverbs 18:22 (NKJV) demonstrates this concept, *"He who finds a wife finds a good thing, and obtains favor from the LORD."* To interpret this correctly, we must realize there are two different ways of interpreting the word *find*. It can mean to put effort into frantically searching or conducting an investigation, or it can mean to happen upon, or to find along the way. Not everything a person finds comes as a result of searching for it. When I was a young boy I was walking down the side of the road and found three dollars lying in the ditch. I wasn't looking for three dollars; I just happened upon it while I was walking. Nevertheless, I still found it.

In studying the original text, I cannot find anything that

absolutely concludes that the word *finds* that is used in Proverbs 18:22 is meant solely for one or the other types of finding; it could be used either way. The word, as used here, is a translation from the Hebrew word matsa' (maw-tsaw'); a primitive root; properly, to come forth to, i.e. appear or exist; transitively, to attain, i.e. find or acquire; figuratively, to occur, meet or be present. When we look at how the word was used throughout the Bible, it has been used both ways. So, we then must look to other Scriptures in order to discover which way to interpret this word. One such clarifying Scripture would be 1 Corinthians 7:35 that defines biblical singleness as having **undistracted** devotion to serving God. If God really wanted a person to search for the person he or she is to marry, how could they also follow the instructions of 1 Corinthians 7:35? When it becomes an individual's responsibility to find their specific person, the natural inclination ends up being that there would be no rest until the search was over. This sounds like a major distraction to me! So in light of this Scripture, I wouldn't interpret the word "find" in Proverbs 18:22 as searching. Therefore, think of finding a wife more as a surprise discovery along the way, as a by-product of following God's plan for your life, rather than as the result of an effort put into searching.

One further reason that the first definition is not suited for use in this Scripture is because, rather than putting God in charge, it puts us in control. I have seen many people taking liberty with this Scripture to suit their own purposes by claiming that *finding a wife* indicates she must be searched for. This serves as justification for doing whatever they want to, instead of what God desires.

This principle of faith is illustrated in Mark, chapter four, in the parable of The Sower. Mark 4:26-27 tells us, *"He also said, 'This is what the kingdom of God is like. A man scatters seed on the ground. Night and day, whether he sleeps or gets up, the seed sprouts and grows, though **he does not know how'"** (emphasis added). Here we are given an illustration of what the kingdom of heaven is like. It is like a man scattering seed on the ground. After he plants it, it doesn't matter if he sleeps or is awake, the seed sprouts and the man doesn't have to even know how it does that. The farmer doesn't have to know exactly how it works, he just knows that it will. It is not knowing how or when God will bring us together with our mate that makes it happen; we just have to trust that He will.

We can all be tempted to create our own scenario on how or when we will someday meet the person God has for us. But, unless God lets us know ahead of time how it will happen, we are only wasting our time and effort to figure that out on our own. As difficult as it may be, it is far better to leave that story blank and allow God to fill those blanks in.

Flirting With Disaster

I have seen plenty of times where people think they have heard from God, when they actually haven't. They are often deceived by the strong emotions that are created for someone who is not a part of God's plan, when he/she does not practice physical abstinence and emotional purity. We can avoid this by treating **all** members of the opposite gender the way we would treat a natural brother or sister. This allows a person to remain physically and emotionally pure without creating desires that stem from the emotions of physical pleasure and not from God's leading. *"Treat younger women as sisters, with absolute purity"* (1 Timothy 5:2). The Phillips translation says, *"with purity and **no more**"* (emphasis added). Job proclaims in Job 31:1, *"I made a covenant with my eyes not to look lustfully at a girl,"* Then, in Proverbs 4:23, we find *"guard your heart…"* All of these Scriptures advise that a person should neither give special time nor attention to a person they will never marry.

When I was a Single Adults pastor, I counseled different members of the group who became involved in a relationship, and afterward asked God if that person was their specific person or not. It is very difficult to hear from God when you build a relationship in that order. Once the relationship has already begun, so has the emotional attachment. These people had already created a desire for a particular person by giving him/her special time and attention. It had become extremely difficult for them to hear from God at this point. I watched as those people struggled through that, and found it to be painful for them. To accurately hear from God, a person must be willing to accept whatever answer God gives. Unfortunately, already being in a relationship before asking God's direction makes a person partial to wanting only to hear a yes from Him.

Undue Influence or Pressure

The revelation of who someone's mate is needs to come to both persons involved. It is not enough for one person to receive the revelation; **both** parties are entitled to receive the benefit of their own revelation. Whoever receives the revelation first should not disclose the news to the future mate until that person has also received their personal revelation from God. If they share that information it will only make it more difficult for that person to discern the will of God, by placing undue influence or pressure on them. **That type of distraction must be avoided**. He/she needs to hear it directly from God himself. True love will not want to steal the beauty of this comforting assurance coming directly from the Father.

Of course, the next question is how does someone know when the other person has their revelation, since the two parties are not supposed to tell each other? My answer: They must use the same God-given patience that got them to this point. They must not let go of that patience because of the excitement and expectations they are now facing due to this future relationship. As for how they know when the other person knows, this is another job for God. He will let them know when the time is right. As you see, everything I am telling you forces the person to be dependent on God, and that is a very good thing!

Instructions for Parents

As parents we must honor the fact that God has a specific person for our child to marry. It is not our responsibility to pick a mate for our child any more than it is your child's. Parents do not have special rights above God in that decision. The choice of whom to marry should be left up to God alone! We must trust that God's choice is the best possible one for our child and we cannot make a better choice. Our desire should be for our child to marry that one specific person of His choosing.

Parents must also understand that it is impossible for us to receive our child's mate revelation for him or her. Our job is not to hear from God for our children, but it is to prepare them to hear for themselves. As we are trusting God for this revelation to take place in our children, we also must expect Him to let us know who it is our child is to marry. This is not for the purpose of us informing our child of God's desire, but to be able to confirm it after our child has approached us with their revelation. At no point in this process should parents try to manipulate and control their child.

It is entirely possible for parents to receive this revelation **before** their child does. If the parents receive the revelation first, as difficult as it may be, they must not inform their child of this news. In that situation it is wise for the parent to not share that information with their child. It is best if that information comes to the child from God directly and not from an external source. Always keep in mind that it must be your child's personal revelation that causes them to make that decision of whom they are to marry.

Once a child has received his or her revelation of whom they are to marry, it is then their responsibility to inform their parents of that fact. At that point the parents may or may not be aware of who God's choice is. If they don't know, it is their responsibility as parents to now seek God as to whether their child has accurately heard from Him or not. The parents' role is to help their child know that they have accurately heard from God.

Parents—Guard Your Heart

Parents can hinder their own ability to hear from God when they bias themselves toward a certain individual of their own choosing and not God's. The danger of this takes place when parents lean to their own understanding and not to God's leading. This can happen when parents allow themselves to be swayed by a person's resume, such as social status or even good character qualities, to determine if that person is God's choice for their child. Those traits alone should not be used as a substitute for God's leading. Anything that does not come as a result of God's leading should not be used to determine who God's choice is.

As parents we can manufacture our own self-created desires for the person we want our child to marry apart from God's plan. We can create our own desires by giving positive time and attention to candidates without hearing from God first. We can create our own preferences by searching for a mate for our child or by trying to guess who our child's mate will be. We can become self-deceived into thinking we have heard from God by doing this. Remember, whatever or whoever we give positive time and attention to we will have a desire for.

When that happens, parents are bound to try and influence their child away from God's choice. I realize it may be difficult for some parents not to do this, because the temptation for this may come from a loving desire to see their children married. This, however, is not a loving way of making it happen.

To prevent that from happening, we as parents must also guard our hearts against creating our own desires apart from God's plan. Everything I have previously discussed in this chapter about what a person should do to guard their heart, in order to not create desires apart from God for their future spouse, is not only applicable to your child, but also to his/her parents.

CHAPTER 10

MARRIAGE PREPARATION: WHILE YOU ARE WAITING

Belief #7

Following God's plan for your life before marriage **prepares** you for marriage. As we begin reading in Genesis 2:18, we find that God intends for Adam to be married, even though at that point, Eve had not yet been created. *"The LORD God said, 'It is not good for **the man** to be alone. I will make a helper suitable for him'"* (emphasis added). What is important to note is the order in which God took action to make Adam's marriage take place after saying this. The very first thing God did after this decision was not to create Eve, because there was something God wanted Adam to do first. Adam had to complete the assignment He gave him in Genesis 2:19-20: *"Now the LORD God had formed out of the **ground** all the beasts of the field and all the birds of the air. He brought them to **the man** to see what he would name them; and whatever **the man** called* *each living creature, that was its name. So **the man** gave names to all the livestock, the birds of the air and all the beasts of the field. But for Adam no suitable helper was found"* (emphasis added). As preparation for his marriage God gave Adam an assignment to name the animals.

Marriage Preparation

Why did God have Adam name all of the animals before He made Eve? Why didn't He make Eve first? It was because Adam had to first follow the part of God's plan for his life prior to marriage. Following God's plan played an important role in Adam's preparation for marriage. If we skip ahead to verse twenty-three, we can read that Adam recognized Eve as being his rib by referring to her as flesh of his flesh and bone of his bones. *"The man said, 'This is now bone of my bones and flesh of my flesh; she shall be called "woman," for she was taken out of man'"* (Genesis 2:23). By Adam having a relationship with God and hearing His voice, it daily trained him to be able to receive revelation from God. Adam had previously learned discernment by naming all the animals; the same type of discernment he needed to recognize Eve as his wife.

While You Are Waiting

This leads us to the question people should be asking nowadays, and that is: What should a person be doing while waiting for the moment God brings him or her together with their future mate? Should they put their life on hold and stand patiently by their front door waiting for their future spouse to show up? No! While a person is waiting for God to reveal who that specific person is, they should be doing works of service for the Lord. *"I would like you to be free from concern. An unmarried man is concerned about the Lord's affairs—how he can please the Lord. But a married man is concerned about the affairs of this world—how he can please his wife—and his interests are divided. … I am saying this for your own good, not to restrict you, but that you may live in a right way in undivided devotion to the Lord"* (1 Corinthians 7:32-35). The Amplified Bible puts it this way: The single person should serve God with undivided, undistracted devotion to the Lord.

One area where I see people make a mistake is thinking they have done all they could do by not dating anyone at all, that somehow that alone is sufficient. But, it is more than not dating, there is much more to the equation than that. This is a two part equation; it is not only what you don't do that matters, it is also what a person does instead. The Bible instructs us on both. God created life to function in a certain way; there are no shortcuts or ways of bypassing His intent. Everything He commands us to do has a reason behind it.

Maturing takes place by doing works of service with undivided, undistracted devotion for the Lord, which is ministering to the needs of others, by doing selfless acts. God doesn't give us a calling in our life only to complete a task. Our callings are multipurpose, not only does the job get done, but doing the job also causes us to grow spiritually. Everyone needs to obey God's assignments of servanthood and selflessness, but for those who are single, it becomes an essential part of their marriage preparation. There is no substitute for living selflessly by meeting the needs of other people and looking for opportunities to serve the Lord. Such actions are what will cause a person to grow. This is for the single person's own good, as mentioned in verse thirty-five. My admonishment is to become as spiritually mature as you can before you find the person God wants you to marry. Being a blessing rather than a curse is a lot more fun, and is the loving thing to do!

The greatest distraction from this type of devotion to the Lord that is faced by single people of all ages, both young and old, is male/female relationships not ordained of God. This is the devil's #1 weapon used against Christian singles. We see this happen when someone becomes totally distracted from their relationship with God because he/she is either in a relationship with someone that God never intended for them to marry, or they are continually seeking and searching to be in that type of relationship. Therefore, they don't have time for their relationship with God, or to do His work, because their lives are consumed with the pursuit of those competing relationships.

People often waste many valuable years of their life going from one relationship to another as their way of searching after a mate, because they believe it is their responsibility to do so, when, in fact, that actually belongs to God. Such misuse of time is not only harmful to their relationship with God, but also to their future marriage relationship. Often without realizing it, they are being unfaithful to a future spouse. When they do this, they are not preparing themselves for marriage. Instead, they are practicing behavior that will be harmful to their future marriage. Knowing God has a specific person for someone to marry means there is no need to spend any time sorting through the masses to produce their own choice of the person they should marry.

Living without having undivided, undistracted devotion to the Lord robs a single person of having an on-fire deep, personal relationship with Him. I have seen this happen over and over. People who at one time were on fire for God get dragged away from His purposes to follow after a relationship not ordained by Him. It is so sad. Jonah 2:8 tells us, *"Those who cling to worthless idols forfeit the grace that could be theirs."* An idol is anything, even a relationship, which is more important to a person than God. Idols consume our time, thought, and energy that actually belong to God. God's grace is available to provide something much better, but people sometimes settle for a substitute and forfeit that grace. The story of Samson and Delilah is a good example of this tragedy.

Unfortunately, some people are deceived into being distracted by purposely not wanting to wait for the specific person God has for them. They have believed a lie that says, "If you are not actively searching and seeking after relationship, after relationship, then you are not interested in getting married. But this is so far from the truth! It is by waiting for and trusting that God will provide a mate that proves a person is committed to having a successful marriage. They are the ones serious about marriage and are willing to go the extra mile. Those people will not be wasting time with relationships not ordained of God. Now they have the valuable time needed to prepare for marriage. It is actually those who are unwilling to wait that have the lesser desire.

Once a person has settled this issue in their own heart the fight may not be over, they are often faced with pressure from others who have the unbiblical viewpoint they at one time held. When a person is not supportive of another person's God-honoring decision to wait for the specific person God has for them, that person puts themselves in a position of opposing God's will for the other person's life.

There is a choice to be made: either he or she will spend time searching for a mate, or they can have undivided, undistracted devotion to the Lord; a person can't do both. We are instructed in Matthew 6:33, *"But seek first his kingdom and his righteousness, and all these things will be given to you as well."*

Looking Toward the Future

One day those of you who are not currently married will be able to find out who your mate is. On that day you want to be able to declare your faithfulness to them. We must all understand that a declaration of faithfulness is not always a declaration of perfection. Even if a person has already made mistakes in this area, it's never too late to commit to be faithful from now on! However, it is important not to hide any unfaithfulness one may have had from the other person; but they both should be able to acknowledge it and put it in the past.

A person can, therefore, boldly and unashamedly, declare their faithfulness to another person, knowing they have made their past right with God and have truly had a change of heart. Although, it must not be merely words spoken, there must be evidence to this commitment of being faithful. This evidence would come from having a time period of absolute faithfulness, regardless of what that time may be. Obviously, the longer the better, thereby demonstrating a true change of heart. They must distance themselves from their last act of unfaithfulness. Oh, and while you are waiting, serve God wholeheartedly!

One day you will be able to find out who your mate is. On that day you want to be able to look them right in the eye and say to them, "I considered you to be so special that I waited faithfully for you. God has been, and will continue to be, my #1 priority. I have served Him faithfully while I waited for you, so that I could become the person He wanted me to be. Now I can be the greatest blessing I can possibly be to you." Until you find out who your specific person will be, you can be faithful to them right now.

For additional resources, please visit:
www.singlepurposeministries.org